Scattered Green Galaxies Press
Falls Church, VA 22042
Copyright © 2014

Publication Data

Still We Rise / poetryN.O.W. Youth Poets

ISBN-13: 978-0991199211
ISBN-10: 0991199219

BISAC: POE001000//Anthologies (multiple authors)

poetryN.O.W. presents

Still We Rise

an anthology of youth poetry

all poems were written
during the 2013-2014 school year
and are original works created
and edited by
the members of poetryN.O.W. clubs

in honor of dr maya angelou

poetryN.O.W. would like to thank all club sponsors and coaches for not only their help in making this anthology a reality, but also for their continued encouragement, support, and dedication to the young people that make this program possible

our deepest gratitude to rachel olarinde (sponsor falls church high school) and scattered green galaxies press for publishing our first anthology

special thanks to all the junior editors from each school who compiled and edited these poems

thank you to zanasha findley (12th grade falls church high school) for our wonderful cover design

and finally, to all who have contributed to the anthology: we sincerely appreciate your hard work, creativity, and commitment to poetry

Table of Contents

Washington and Lee- Arlington, VA

Teachers by *Pooyan Kimiyaee*
Iranian Freedom by *Pooyan Kimiyaee*
That's Not A Religion by *Hanan Seid*
Counting Sheep by *Hanan Seid*
Africa by *Milen Mehari*
I Love God by *Grace Leckey*
Mentally Energetic by *Nathan Nisenson*
Broken Bones by *Nathan Nisenson*
From A Girlfriend by *Grace Burgess*
Eyes by *James Markert*
Advice to Yourself by *James Markert*

T.C Williams- Alexandria, VA

Moon Love by *Eboni Reid*
A Cigarette and Juliette by *Amir Shareak*
Mural by *Jalisa Orellana*
Juliet by *Jalisa Orellana*
Gymnopistim by *Patrick Ensslin*
Spiegel I'm Spiegel by *Patrick Ensslin*
Greek Tragedy by *Frankie Amero*
Fear by *Frankie Amero*
Adolescence by *Siem Sium*
My Confession by *Sydney Dively*
The Warmest Winter Ever by *Yonas Araya*

West Springfield- Springfield, VA

She is living the Struggle by *Brooke Parsons*
Sticks and Stones by Dorothy *Adu-Amankwah*
Little Girl (Letters of the past and the present me) by *Dorothy Adu-Amankwah*
This War Torn World by *Brandon VanderLaan*
The Caged Bird is Me by *Brooke Parsons*
A Soul Like Mine by *Brandon VanderLaan*
The so called "sister" by *Hannah Kim*

Falls Church High School- Falls Church, VA

I'm Not a Poet by *Zanasha Findley*
It's Ok by *Zanasha Findley*
Love Child by *Danny Tran*
I'm Not Ready by *Isaiah Abadia*
The Color Brown by *Isaiah Abadia*
I Love You by *Jason Reales*
1, 2, 3 by *Mikalanne Paladino*
Curry Stain by *Mikalanne Paladino*

Chantilly High School- Chantilly, VA

Standing on the Ocean by *Lina Snyder Romero*
Sorry I'm Not You by *Lina Snyder Romero*

Hayfield Secondary School- Alexandria, VA

Seasick by *Sam Dickison*
Untitled by *Sam Dickison*
Metamorphosis by *Judy Russell*
The edge of earth *by Judy Russell*

Washington and Lee High School
Arlington, VA

Teachers by Pooyan Kimiyaee

I was a dilapidated man
Shackled in the midst of tidal waves
caused by the gravity of my rebellious behavior
He is a man haunted by the past.
He Never finished high school
but went on to become a journalist
He is my superhero
He is my father
I always felt safe with him
Respected him
Trusted him
Loved him

As a teenager I never felt compelled to rebel against
him
Because he told me that I was the best thing that ever
happened to him;
That I was more than a broken toy
rotting away in the attic

He is in jail now
I guess freedom of speech isn't exactly a thing in Iran
when it comes to religion and apparently you are
considered a part of "religion"
While my father taught me about love and acceptance
you had a different approach
Your methods could be summed up in a quote from the
greatest man who never lived:
"You are not special;
You are not a beautiful and unique snowflake;

You are the same decaying organic matter as everyone
else
And we are the all singing, all dancing crap of the
world"

You taught me all must be sacrificed in the name of
Allah -
if he demands it

Your noxious deception
overflowing
your eyes;
your words;
your clothes;
and I see as my friends drop like the leaves of the
autumn tree
I shout as the color green becomes the symbol of your
greatest fear
Among the falling leaves of trees,
and the deathly sensation of the cold breeze
I will rise higher to fall harder

But even with my broken wings I refuse to sacrifice
myself for your lies
I will not bow down
Because you lied,
You killed,
You raped,
and you spat in the face of what humanity you had left
You played frisbee with the halo around your head
You took away my innocence

Your words;
like bullets that rip me apart day after day
and the only thing keeping me alive is that they know;
The People see you for what you are
and you can't lie to them anymore.

You are a moribund man
Drowning in oceans of distrust,
because of the gravity
of my rebellious behavior.

Iranian Freedom by Pooyan Kimiyaee

I am a dead poet.
The ghost of a poet violated in the street.
My wings were ripped apart,
left lying bloody in the snow
and I was left to freeze
with the shackles and chains
binding me to the ground.

I am a Prisoner.
My guards are ambitious;
they aspire to hide their devilish intentions behind
delicate masks of religion
as they leave my body walked all over.

I was a poem.
On the white paper with blue lines.
I felt immortalized by the black ink,
but when I was torn apart
my meaning flew away
into the void of thought.

I am a soldier fallen from grace after war.
My glamorous return is pointless.
I lay in the grass;
jobless; wingless; mindless; weightless; helpless;
restless;
flawed.
I break.

Madness seizes control over my mind—
I am an orphan.

Enraged and adopted.
I can easily observe the sympathy
in my protector's eyes;
hear it in every word.
I know they understand;
everybody understands.
But only for a while.
After that,
they start expecting the angry little kid to do
something he knows he can't do:
to move on.

I was a corpse.
Left headless on the ground; I froze.
My blood spilled on the snow became
eye-candy to those who executed me in the name of
"Freedom."

I am a Poem.
Flooded with metaphors and grotesque imagery.
Vaunting of my misery to maintain an inspiring visage.

I am the Rebel's washed up graffiti.
The Soldier's poem.
The shout of decried women.
I am the philanthropic philosophy
of a journalist in chains.
I am the artist's portrait of the all seeing,
all hearing Big Brothers of this nation
On the walls of every single classroom.

I am the fear of the color green.
I am a banned western philosophy.

I was just an idea;
an idea which would not be muted;
an idea that stood up against the scum who stole my
voice.
And I am gone because you wouldn't listen.
I died in the streets because you stood
and watched from the safety of your window.
I died.
Not as a man,
nor a symbol,
but as Freedom—
resurrected through this poem
so you would never forget.

That's Not a Religion by Hanan Seid

It's crazy how 3 numbers can turn me from a friend
to a flight threat —
like I had the ability to turn my watch
to a bomb set.
And any time I spoke an Arabic phrase
they would all look so afraid,
like saying 'assalamu alaykum' was code for "lets blow
up the place."
And I apologize for the 19 inhumane,
but note that 99% of us are sane.

Maybe I'm overreacting;
honestly, what country would take the actions of a few
and blame it on a whole civilization?
Thank God we don't live in that nation.

No,
I live in the land of the free
sworn up and down for both you and me,
but freedom is tested throughout history
so forgive me if I don't see —
too blind and deaf to see sanity,
and never hear reality in a land where freedom
doesn't really come free...

Stares;
screaming whispers
and pity.
Anytime a teacher brings up New York City
I'm labeled.
Organized on the media's table.

"Those muslims are so unstable."
Fighting in armies against peace.
The more of us, the more crime rates increase.
3,000 deceased.

And I apologized numerous times,
even though I know it had nothing
to do with me.

You call me that girl with the veil that's oppressed
but when you see a nun walk around you give her the
utmost respect.

But I want you to get to know me,
and what I believe.
Don't let them twist your mind; they deceive.
Don't trust everything that is said —
all the media wants is hatred to be spread,
and tomorrow
I'll introduce you to my scarlet letter.

When I was a little girl I never walked next to my
mother because of how others viewed her.
They didn't even know who we were.

All those stares,
all those words
never phased her.
All I wanted was to be from here.
But swearing to this country would mean I was to
forget I'm from there

How do you forget what brought you here in the first place?
It's like looking at my ma' and saying what you are is a waste.

I'm from here today:
all the struggles, all the history that goes through my veins, is no more than just history.
Now that's insane,
but today I tell them I'm from there,
and I say it proudly
'cause these ignorant idiots don't know anything about me.

Now try not to see what is seen and listen to me:
there is terrorism, and there are terrorists living, but I'm here to remind you that that's not a religion. I pity the media because their minds need help; love me or hate, just as long as you do it by yourself. I break stereotypes on a daily basis. A slick worded hijabi Ohhh —you should have seen their faces. So when I introduce myself tomorrow I want you to know me, and not the preconceived idea of me.

Counting Sheep by Hanan Seid

You can't hide your flaws
in such an open place.
Or any of your scars
beneath that plastic face.
Because wounds go deeper than just blood —
wounds go inside and create a flood that will wash
down all of your days,
and as long as it stays,
you won't feel the same.

You sit and watch commercials in hopes
for a cure.
Something new.
Something pure.

"Cymbalta can help,"
it starts to say.
Help in what way?
Help with the feeling of being alone?
Even when surrounded with people you know?

As you sit,
silence creeps up your sleeve,
like little goosebumps,
making its way up to your head.

You feel silence in such a crowded place.
Your mind starts to race as you start to talk, but never
say a word.
Tears coming down your face,
but can anyone see you in the rain?

Help with the pressure to look a certain way?
That would mean this pill can change society's
judgmental ways.
But you know that humanity's nature can't be changed.

And if every word in every song were rearranged,
you'd see that everybody's popping pills,
and they call you deranged.

Help with memories of your childhood?
This pill has the power to erase
but, come on —
even that can't be replaced.
After all that you have faced,
life is no roller coaster:
it's a race.

Help with your inability to sleep?
Even after counting sheep
your head goes back;
pain is stacked;
1 sheep, 2 sheep, 3...
can your pill help me?
Help with not wanting to stay?
'Cause you're tired of feeling the pain;
tired of all the blood stains that come out of your veins.

Who knew that living was worse than dying?
Who knew that pain was more powerful than any
bullet?

And who knew that being alone in a prison you create
was the same as playing Russian Roulette in your
head?—
Will you come out or will you be dead?

'Lonely' is a weapon of mass destruction.
A term that's used too easily.
It vigorously ricochets in your head.
Your pill can't help with that
Your pill can't help with millions of girls, wishing that
there stomachs were flat
Cymbalta can't help,
not with that

Africa by Milen Mehari

I am the African spirit
willing to speak the truth
our school systems only breeze through
Please don't think I have sass
for informing the children of today
what really happened in their past.

It always goes the same way
Greece, Italy. The Romans and the Greeks
were taught to me in the class called history.

Teach me about Nefertiti
not just the dirty streets that I roam, and call home.
You told me that Rome was home to the greatest
nation,
Empire, but fail to mention the tombs of the Nubians.
Call me unique.. Tell me I'm exotic, just don't say freak.

If I could unveil the mystery
that is called black history
i would first mention how..
We were kings and queens once!
Ruled the seas, skies, and all who roamed

Until europeans came
and tore us from our homes
Separating me from my entire family.
I was put on the boat
I traveled until I was finally made
to bow down and work on the ground.

Through withholding education and degradation
I was made to feel much worse than unworthy
But how can I be impure if I grow your food?

My blood of my oppression fertilizes the soil
That nourishes your body!
How can I be less than you
if I am keeping you alive?

I asked these questions now
for my ancestors who can not

These thoughts move
with great emotion inside my head..
keeping me awake through the nights.
Despite the sadness they cause
they keep me warm because
when your history is cloaked in mystery
you're left to find refuge within your own mind.

This is not a poem to blame
Rather resurrect a proud history
from the shadows, textbooks
not written by or for us

It's not a mystery that
we all do wrong
and we can improve it.
but first we much change course with stealth
to insure that history doesn't repeat itself

I am the new face of Africa.

No, I'm not hungry,
except for success
but I am what is,
what was, and what should be known
as the true tale of black history.

I Love God by Grace Leckey

I Love God.
I love God, I really do
I'm into saying rosaries and giving blessings.
But when I recite scripture without a filter,
people look at me funny...
And I don't blame them —
because this is just what nine years of Catholic school
looks like

It is weird to come across a girl like me;
straight out of central casting for an innocent private
school child,
and some people just don't know what to do
with the influx of psalms, and the holy righteous
vibes...
But I don't blame them!
It is "weird,"
but there's a twist:
On the one hand,
I wear a cross everyday
and recommend saints to ask for intercession,
but on the other
I'm just a kid.

So,
do you believe me?

Now... I'm Catholic.
I'm Catholic and I love being Catholic
because the word means Universal.
But Catholic is a scary word now,

associated with conservative, exclusive ways of life
and a deeply flawed hierarchy
that breaks the hearts of her people.
But such a towering mistake
will give way like houses foolishly built on sand instead
of rock
Sound familiar?

Now, I do not intend to shove conversion
and a savior down anyone's throat,
but for the sake of a pure poem...

Jesus hung out with
widows, and orphans, and teenagers, and prostitutes,
and, shepherds, and thieves;
His disciples were wild— but wild and free.
And if God came right now
She'd say hello to you,
and you, and to all the wanderers,
and band geeks, and the gamers, and the hipsters who
aren't hipsters, and the poets and the basketball
players, and the songwriters,
because that is Universal Love.

So yes, I go to church
and I say, "Praise The Lord, Jerusalem!" out loud &
quite frequently.
But I promise a twist:
when you see me do the sign of the cross
 it is NOT "In the name of the men, the white people,
and the heterosexuals—"
God Save the people!
No;

It's the name of change and justice from
She who is master of the sky
and it's a radical idea to me,
and to you,
and to my sisters and brothers who identify as
Catholic, too.

But the idea that being a religious person means
believing only what some priest has to say on
gay marriage,
immigration,
and birth control
has to be defenestrated.

What side of the aisle you feel comfortable on
is up to you.

Catholic means universal;
don't let any man in fancy robes convince you
otherwise.
Religions shouldn't draw lines,
they should paint rainbows.
And in Jericho and Israel and Jerusalem,
God's Prophets were just a couple radical slam poets
themselves.

Mentally Energetic by Nathan Nisenson

Every morning I lock my mind away into the narrow
world of focused thinking
and force it to labor in the fields of attentive behavior.

A tiny, beige, unsuspecting pill tells my brain what to
think and how to think about it.
I am forced into thinking about what's "important",
like school and assignments.
I consider everything else as secondary;
imagination is trivial, and daydreaming is unimportant.
Math tests aren't passed with creativity,
so I have no choice but to disregard it.

My mind is in prison but every weekend it escapes.
It runs free into a world of things that haven't been
invented,
surrounded by people that don't exist.

My thoughts feel like they're on fire
As I run through fields of the fourth primary color,
living in a world with buildings 100 stories deep.
I look at things as what they could be
because normal is never good enough

Every weekend my mind is free,
and every Monday morning, week after week,
it is imprisoned again.

On weekdays I'm back to work;
my mind is a computer
calculating algebra rather creating than alien planets,

concerned with symmetrical parabolas and not shifts in
gravity.
I have no choice but to focus on the worksheet on top
of my desk
instead of the adventures inside of my head
that I constantly crave to crawl back into.

But that constant whirring goes on
long after the school day ends
and with no math problems left to answer
I'm forced to find something else to question:
I question the trophies on my wall
and whether I truly deserve them.
I think about my doctor
and whether he knows whats its like to be "chemically
imbalanced,"
and I ask what gives him the right
To tell me how I should feel.

I am not the only one with my thoughts relentlessly
tethered
to things that other people find important.
Statistically speaking, 1 in 10 of you is prescribed a
psychoactive drug.
We are part of a generation of kids,
labeled from infancy by men in white suits,
people who call themselves doctors
but act more like salesmen,
telling kids they have something wrong with them,
teaching them to believe that a pill would make
everything better
and preaching the belief that
being average and being cured are the same thing.

My mind is in prison with 2 million cellmates.
yes, there are people that see this prison as a sanctuary
there are people who need these pills,
but there are countless others who don't
Kids who are growing up thinking that they need to be
fixed
when they were never broken in the first place

Why did we become like this?
when did we start thinking
that just because a child's mind wanders to far off
places
that we are obligated to shackle it to the ground
was it because of test scores?
Profit margins?

This is more than a trend,
this is more than a craze.
This is a disease we don't even know we have
because its been killing us so slowly
and for so long,
that today over medication seems as normal as the
sunrise

Our country has created a system
that knows children only by their flaws,
classifies them with jargon,
and measures them by milligrams.

We force away the flaws in our children
through tiny, beige, unsuspecting pills.
They are filled with combinations of chemicals

to match whatever quirk or characteristic
or personality
that they are meant to hide.

My pill is called Adderall.
It's called a stimulant
It's called a cure
But it isn't.
It's a set of crutches
that have never let me learn how to walk,
a blank mask
that has become more familiar than my own face.
It is life raft that i want to leave,
but can't,
because I'm afraid that
I've forgotten how to swim.

Broken Bones by Nathan Nisenson

When I was 7 years old I broke my arm and gashed my forehead
after tripping on a rock no taller than 2 inches.
The next week I received 18 signatures on my cast.
I felt famous.
The day after, I saw a kid eating lunch alone in the corner
he had a bowl cut, a stutter in his speech, and no friends
I saw him there everyday,
and I wondered if he knew that all he needed to do to make friends
was to fall out of a tree.

As years went on,
I realized that I wasn't the one in pain that day.
Kids feel bad for those with casts and crutches,
and I used to idolize those bandaged veterans for their tenacity and strength,
but it's the kids in the corner—
the rejects, the misfits, and the weirdos,
that know this pain better than anyone.

The only difference is that no one can see their scars;
these kids have to hide under a mask of silence.
While sticks and stones may not break their bones,
words will always hurt them.

We need to help them,
but we place the burden
on people who can't:

The peacekeepers of schools—
the kind hearted mentors;
teachers intervene in bullying only 4% of the time.
They can't save everyone.
There are people who can,
but they don't.
One in every four parents says that being bullied builds
character,
but a sledgehammer does not make a wall stronger,
it only chips away piece by piece
until something gives way.

We say that its not our problem,
that kids will be kids;
we say that they can speak out and fight back,
but these children are not willing soldiers—
they are prisoners of war in their own country;
victims of a battle that people are too ashamed to talk
about.

I have seen this conflict take lives
I know the pain of these victims because I was one of
them;
I have never broken a bone in my body;
I was not the kid that tripped on a rock—
I was the kid in the corner
that dreamed of falling out of a tree.

I always thought that this was just how things were,
that high-school was supposed to be like this.
But I was wrong.
This system is wrong.
Childhood does not have to entail agony;

there is no graduation requirement for misery;
high-school does not need to leave students warped
and angry at the world.

If we stopped making bullying out to be a fact of life,
and admit that it is a disease,
then maybe we can start to fix it.
Maybe we could try to cure it

From A Girlfriend by Grace Burgess

I know I'm just the opening act.
I'm just warming you up
for what's coming down the line.
I'm not the one you've been
waiting for all this time

I know my time's shorter,
That I'm just here to get you ready
to love her better
when the time comes.
But that doesn't mean you can't sing along
while this lasts.

And when your mouth moves in time with hers
Just remember
I taught you what lip gloss tastes like
When you reach for her hand
Keep in mind
I showed you what connection felt like
When you tell her that you love her
please don't forget
who wrote the first song,
the one that told you what love meant.

Eyes by James Markert

Eyes
These are not just simple eyes
These are orbs of light
These are pools of shadows
They are the guardians of the soul

These are a gift to us
A gift we bear with a weight
A gift of being able to see
The weight of love and hate

The freedom of turning these spheres
From here to there and being able to see, to perceive
Allows us to move about without any fears
Allows us to see what we before could not conceive

The light coming from elsewhere to enter our eyes
Just to simply bounce off and dance away
Uncaring for whether the eye smiles or cries
But shining forth at the start of each new day

As light flees and day crawls to night
The merry dance of the eye's light fades away
And arrives the minister of man's plight
Calling forth the mind's shadowy king to play

When crowned by either Day's light or Night's plight
The two stand still and strong forever so long
Never embracing the fire or ice of Day and Night
But serving to let man stand aside and Sing his Song.

Advice To Yourself by James Markert

Wherever you are, whenever you are reading this
know that it is just me, yourself, writing this to speak
out to you
A younger speaking to the older through words written
on this day

Remember when you went out to the back of the house
to sit on the hill
Only seeking an escape from the script and stress of
this world
To feel the cool grass under your feet
And to sit on the ground and cry

Then remember when once you were done crying you
laid back
turning your eyes to the sky
watching as two birds chased each other through the
sky
As the spider checked his web in the tree high above
for the night
All as the light slowly faded away and lightning bugs
rose up to dance

Finally, remember when your frown slowly grew into a
smile
And when you had only been weeping a minute ago
You began to laugh

The reason why is because when you had been crying
You had been oblivious to the world around you

Nature, a beautiful world made both by beasts and men
Then when you stopped being sad and laid back you then could see
As you were no longer blinded by yourself and were happy

More simply put, you realized you are human
and being so cannot achieve everything at once
But you can choose to believe and hold faith in what you choose

This leads to my advice to you.
Choose whatever you want to be and whatever you want to believe in
But remember, don't blind yourself to the beautiful world around you
Enjoy your time with your family and friends
Get your work done and unburden yourself of the stress
Lastly, stop lying to yourself
You are neither sorrow nor joy
you are human.

(Ps: Don't stay out too long b/c the mosquitoes are a pain in the back)

**T.C. WILLIAMS HIGH SCHOOL
ALEXANDRIA, VIRGINIA**

Moon Love by Eboni Reid

We're in a generation where souls are lost
Drifting away from the bright spaces of our thoughts
Aimlessly trying to capture the faint appearances
of the things we block out
when the sun is high on Its throne
Looking down on us with galaxies and planets in
between to keep the distance
from our over exploring minds apart

Terrified that on day we might overcome and venture
out beyond the distance of light into the darkness
where our thoughts are appreciated by one that tells us
where there in its gray blue-ish form
One that has arrived with good news
That our labor is done for the day and that our bodies
can relax in the mist of the hot steam from our showers
as the few stars twinkle about from our distance
Because truly the moon is our friend
Our companion that feels the skin ripping from the
knife, leaking the blood that reminds us that we are no
different than the person sitting next to us on the train

at midnight as we carry a bottle of ciroc in our hand
searching for a good time to survive
Surviving the one that they call the Bright King from
forcing us to deal with the horrors of the world
Making us sit through the intense bright holes that
surround us of the Ashley's or the Brad's or the people
just scraping by trying to make a living that is
acceptable

To the opinionated Bright King that sees everything no
matter how thick your blinds are hiding behind your
thick silhouette black curtains
The light spills through

Can't you hear it the constant dripping for the corner
As you pile on paper towel to soak up the mess that the
day has brought
Like a water balloon filled up to capacity it burst
releasing all the horrors that you can imagine only
while your eyes are opened so terrified you have to
close them and think of that one lovely person
To absorb the constant miseries that every female and
male have experienced
To deal with the grief that is

A Cigarette and Juliette by Amir Shareak

The night hours have risen and a blank midnight sheet
has been woven over our heads,
Our new Mother Moon is watching over us in secrecy,
I look up at the vacant black void, cursing suburbia
because she's kept me from seeing the belt of Orion,
"What do you think seeing the stars is like? I bet there's
so many to see,"
The street lamps illuminate so little of you,
The other on the opposing side is flickering,
I wonder if you're even there, but I know you are when
you crash land me from my stargazing venture,
'Pass me my lighter,'
My jacket pocket is the keeper of your miniature torch,
I hand it over and you withdraw your gold and snow
white release,
Your thickened lips part and you nuzzle it between
them,
Flick, flick,
Your French tipped nails struggle, priming the pump of
lighter fluid to create flames,
Flick, flick,
I see your eyebrows fluctuate, arches to narrow,
surprise at first, then anger at the conclusion,
'I think I'm out,'
"Why do you smoke anyway?"
Before both of us, a flame ignites,
Your eyes reflect the twitching ember and your golden
smile appears,
The end of the cigarette quickly turns white to charcoal
and in comes the release,

Out comes the cloud of anger that you've been wanting to dismiss your entire day,
'Why don't you?'
"I don't know. It just never appealed to me,"
'I'm telling you, don't knock it 'til you try it,'
Why must those ripened rose lips touch the gold of the flamed nicotine?
You're not in the mood for my "Cigarettes-are-bad-for-your-health" speech, and I'm not in the mood to give it,
I've known you for 5 years,
I can read you,
Your retaliation gifted to me a minute explanation:
"A pack a day keeps the sadness away,"
Bullshit,
I'm forming arguments with you within my gray matter,
"Don't you know how bad those are on your lungs?"
Yet I'm unable to form the words,
You're the one leaving me breathless,
My expression quickly dims and you take notice,
'What's wrong?'
I can't tell you that you burning away your life upsets me,
Day by day,
"Why do so many say that anyone would be lucky to have me when no one has been 'lucky' enough to stumble across me?"
'I hate hearing you talk like this,'
"It's true,"
'But it isn't, just wait. She's coming,'
"How do you know?"
Your smile reassured me,
It glowed in the street lamps' emissions,

'A girl just knows,'
It was weird, I could feel your smoke rest itself onto me,
I didn't mind it,
"So Oakland, so Oakland,"
"I like your text tone,"
'You know how much I love Childish!'
"The man's a visionary, I swear,"
'Mom's getting anxious...Time to go,'
Our shoes smack from concrete to asphalt in unison,
My hands are cuddling my pockets, and you still can't put that damn cigarette out,
'Hang out in here for a sec,'
It was your mom's car,
The dome light started to dim out the very second our doors locked in place,
'Turn on the radio,'
Pressing the biggest circle, I could feel the initial low tones begin to bellow into my core,
"I was making Japanese while she's watchin' DVDs in Oakland, in Oakland,"
Both of our faces light up and we immediately start to sing along,
We're like little kids again,
You lift the cancer stick up one more time to your puckered lips,
'One more for the road,'
I maneuver my wrist to turn up the nob,
"You know how I get when I'm lonely, I think about you in the moments,"
My eyes lock to yours,
"Shotgun,"

Your perfectly curled lashes elevate from the surprise,
but then slowly descend in that lusty fashion that you
love to do,
You tease,
My chin is enveloped by your finely crafted nails and
your even fingertips,
'Your chin hair is so cute,'
Next thing that I know, our lips finally touch,
From the passenger side, I didn't know how to feel
about my mouth being filled to the brim with a bitter
cloud of anguish,
But there was something about tasting your sweet, soft
lips,
It made it seem as if I could taste the stars that I could
never see.

Mural by Jalisa Orellana

Today I feel cerulean
like oceans.
I feel deep purple,
like blueberries,
like the dark wine of my nails.
I feel slow like grays
and tired like maroons,
I can't always feel golden,
I can't always be polished
Some days I'm dull
Some days I'm matte
Some days I'm chrome.
But today I'm a mural of turquoises
and indigos
spiraling into an indefinite painting
that I hope someone
will deem masterpiece

Juliet by Jalisa Orellana

I wonder,
if I ever work up enough courage
to be your Juliet
would we end up
in the same place?
would you welcome me with a hug so tight that I'd
forget
what my lungs were there for?
or would you be devastated?
upset?
would you feel misunderstood?
as if your not-so-valiant
act of bravery
weren't to be interpreted like this,
would you think I didn't care enough to try anything to
remember your face against mine?
even if it means looking for you in other people
would you think I wouldn't travel across stones on my
knees to try & replicate
the way your hands would cup my hips in a gesture of
comfort
like a mother bear to her cubs
like a man to his wife
like a Romeo to his Juliet
I can't even look up at the stars to try & find you
anymore
I'm done reading horoscopes and searching for
constellations
I'm tired of looking for the guidelines to my life in an
open-ended self-help book

I'm tired of only ever going to sleep when I know I'll
see you there
when my only way of closure are the brief moments I
see you when I close my eyes
& the guilt still drapes itself over me
yet it's still more bearable than the memory of the
hospital clothes draped over your limp body-
than the tubes and wires entering and exiting your
nostrils
than the blood gushing from the gunshot wound to
your head
because I still can't be your heroine and you still refuse
to call for help
I'm tired of trying to recreate Shakespearean tragedies
when I don't care enough to write them on paper
because I can't bear to remember
another lonely Tuesday night's screenplay
with an ending just as sad and abysmal as the original
this is one of the very few instances I'm content with
being cliché
permanently holding a grudge against myself for
letting my pride be our downfall
letting my stubbornness interfere with piecing back
together our masterpiece
I blame myself for letting us fall apart
If I were brave enough to be your Juliet, would we have
ended up in the same place?

Gymnopistim by Patrick Ensslin

when i felt a tugging at my sleeve,
i thought there were a progonist.

and then, when fimmed my rug,
quid hist moriartie's nassionfrut.

my truth was on my chin, my jist
was hanged from my pockitchen.

the lawyer found me in the guddr,
just swinging the dert frm my pants.

i new there were products; i new
kitchenwipes to save the cupberd.

but, but werriors held swerds in the
past, why should it happen now.

we have moovd beyund such things
as this.

This is what we have moovd beyund.

Spiegel Im Spiegel by Patrick Ensslin

A mirror reflecting a
mirror reflecting a
mirror reflecting a
face that I don't know and
you don't know and nobody really
knew but was looking at us from the
corner and through the window, and
under the platform and in the
mirror reflecting a
mirror reflecting an
eye that can't close,
a ceiling moving in circles above our houses at night,
and
in the day, a framework, a clockwork,
a roulette wheel and a ball inside, and
a shower head dripping, and a train
braking, and the noises the birds make in
the morning, the vibrations moving slowly, towards the
wall, the
mirror reflecting a
mirror reflecting a
pupil now, a black thing,
something that looks like it should be
something, but it's only a pit, and a crossroads, and a
stone in a pond, and the palm of a hand, the origin.

Greek Tragedy by Frankie Amero

I know what it feels like:
Words taking the shape of glass breaking,
It sounds like a stiletto through the ribs,
Where some try to keep things caged,
But I cannot contain what was never there,
So I won't spare you the memories,
Of my grandmother cupping her hands beneath my eyes,
Telling me it's okay to cry,
I can learn to paint with those tears,
I won't tell you that everything pushed off a cliff learns how to fly,
Learns to love the sky,
I won't lie and say broken wings carry more than fear,
Because I know,
Whatever name some call you outside of,
You're Pandora:
You'll play me whatever song I like,
But hope is gonna die,
Suffocated by the evils inside,
Unless you open the box,
Trying to pick the locks,
You've got more keys than a keyboard,
But just like music,
Everything starts and ends with C,
Can you see the knife life has been trying to twist you around?
You haven't found redemption for your mistakes,
That faith doesn't bend before it breaks us,
Makes us wish we were something we are not,
But you've got to let go of that Greek fire inside,

Because pride's already burned you so badly,
It kept you from calling save me,
And I can't get mad when the voiceless leave
something unspoken,
I won't leave you broken,
But I can't fix what you don't let me see,
So I need you to give me your envy,
So your worth isn't superseded by less,
Cause half of the world's mess is made when we don't
see our own value,
I need you to give me your illness,
All that stress,
Because you deserve to be healthy,
You see I need you to give me your hate,
You don't have to forget it,
But I don't want you regret it when you finally see the
opportunities you've missed,
Because friend,
You're an artist,
So why don't you take your tears and paint clouds to
chase your blues away,
Paint the sun so that your skies aren't gray,
Paint seeds to set down roots for a better tomorrow,
Paint the whole tree evergreen,
So your smile doesn't leave,
And don't forget that we were born with our hearts on
our sleeves so that when we hurt,
When the pain and the sorrow is too much to bear,
We can reach out to touch,
To be touched,
Because when we feel alone,
Hope is always right here.

Fear by Frankie Emero

Boogie man, Slender man, Fear,
I know you're not a man,
And I'm calling you outside of your name!
I heard you came here to die,
But you better mean like a Phoenix,
Cause I'll drag you back from hell before I let you settle
with the black stripes of an old prison uniform,
The yellow stains of shame left by a child's nightmare,
The knife I've balanced on my wrists more than once,
And I thank god you were never sharp enough to cut
me,
Even though your apathy usually rips lives apart,
Your ribs caging every shattered heart,
When you refuse to remind us that whatever pencil we
hold can become Excalibur,
Because our words are hollow points of a higher
caliber,
Yes Fear,
I'm calling you outside of your name,
But I know you came,
Here after paying the price for lifting countless spirits,
Your back cracked at every vertebra,
Spine less than whole,
Leaving you puzzled,
By the pieces of a broken soul,
And I can't pretend you're not there,
Like you want me to,
Wrists in ribbons,
Your hopes imprisoned,
You are becoming your own worst nightmare,
Feeling just as alone as I did,

Until you pulled me out of the dark,
And held my hand when I was shaky,
Well now you're shaking,
Hands with a devil of your own design,
And I know angels fall every day,
But it's only when they choose to let go,
And even though I've gotten pretty good at catching people,
Fear,
I will not coddle you,
I will not baby a child who has lived longer than anyone I've ever known,
Because everyone needs a big sister now and then,
But sometimes,
Our job is to push until they push back,
So I'm gonna keep calling you outside of your name,
Because that's what you are:
Afraid to remember what a mirror looks like,
To see yourself as the black lines giving meter to music,
To see your yellow rays of sunshine making life a little brighter,
To see that you make everyone's load a little lighter,
Because you are a Queen,
We are your colony,
A cacophony of wings,
That logic says shouldn't be able to fly,
But you're the reason we can defy all reason,
So come on,
Show me what you're made of,
You don't have to stand straight,
Stand strong,
Stand proud,
Cause you're not someone who gets beaten,

Brave,
You are something to be,
And if you can remember how to do it,
Who knows?
Maybe I can too.

Adolescence by Siem Sium

Adolescence is the phase of life
In which a child's thoughts attempt
to dissect abstract ideas.
A child's thoughts
on love, hate, and sorrow will
become increasingly complex.
This phase in life is the prelude to a defined state of mind;
But the demise of youthful thinking
The rise of Maturity.
Yet even the most Mature of
People, will try to fulfill
Either their personal ambitions
Or their unquenchable desires
With the same youthful dreams of
love, sorrow or hate.
To dream of a world of their own.
Sadly, the perfect qualities will never be in place
A single reality may never coexist
With the vast feelings of
a world full of millions.
Yet it's clear to see that we all
Strive for such a reality;
Filled with equal opportunity and voice
A state built on pure ambitions
That may never age to corrupt.
A utopia.
Therefore, perhaps the transition
Between child to grown
Is not just defining the mind
But also to cope with
the youthful dreams
and manage to work
for a better reality.

My Confession by Sydney Dively

Alright it's true.
My infatuation for you was like a shallow lake
It could be seen right through, and there was nothing
deeper than what you saw.
I knew deep down I couldn't handle your obnoxious
jokes, your rude comments of others, or your closed
mind
Everything I felt, was just because of your tall, tan skin,
your blue eyes, your muscles, and your inability to love
me
I thought I wanted you so terribly, and I couldn't sleep
without thinking of what you COULD be
But it was never what you actually were
And that's why I moved on from you so quickly.

The Warmest Winter Ever by Yonas Araya

When I look at her face,
I can see the sunrise to everyday of the rest of my life.
When her lips touch mine I can taste every meal that I
will ever need,
the source of my power, the energy to my being, call me
crazy but this is where I want to be.
When her lips touch mine,
a chill down my spine,
I think, and I hope, that when I call your name in a
screaming whisper, the wind carries the sound of my love
to you leaving me with a deafening silence.
I know that our bodies are young, but our souls are old,
and the winter is cold, but when you touch me I feel your
summertime.
You are an endless book I'll never get tired of reading,
never get tired of turning pages,
I'll use my context clues to figure out your moods
I'll make coffee for me but tea for you
and I promise to put three sugars even though you said
two because,
I know what you meant and I wont pretend
that we arent young and relationships dont end,
I know theres a chance we may split
never marry or have kids,
but theres a fifty-fifty chance that youre my "her" and Im
your "him"
They say we are too young, too young to know what love
is, but they dont understand I want to spend the rest of
my life finding out with you.
I know that life is short,
and even shorter without you,
so I'll lose count of the days in your company,
during the warmest winter ever.

West Springfield High School
Springfield, Virginia

She is Living the Struggle by Brooke Parsons

Her feet hit the end of the post
because her bed is too small

                Her back aches

and moans from
another night of sleeping on the floor
She must wake up early Monday
morning foranother day of school
 She must go to work in the fields
because she is not allowed to learn
Now she is forced to walk
3 feet to the water fountain,
that spits out lukewarm water

                It is 2 miles to the

nearest water
supply, and drought has turned her
water to muddy sludge
The clouds have cleared and
the temperature rises to 86;
shemust retreat inside

                Outside, working,

her skin starts to burn
in the 106 degree sun. She has no
choice but to keep looking for food
Her fridge is full of left overs 2
days old, and there is no mayo
for a sandwich

                She divides a slice

of bread and a bowl of
rice among her three sisters. There is not
enough for all so she must go to bed hungry
again

Sick of left overs, she is forced
to use her allowance to pay
for take out

                              She must sell her

last goat to pay for
vaccines for her sisters, for without
them, they will surly die
She screams in protest about
being taken to the family doctor
because she does not want to get
a shot

                                   She struggles to

survive and raise her sisters
in a city that values her life less than a dog's
She complains about not having
the latest iPhone

She is living "The Struggle"   She is living the
struggle

Sticks and Stones by Dorothy Adu-Amankwah

I wonder who ever gave the idea that,
Sticks and Stones may break your bones,
But words will never hurt you.

If you ever been hurt before,
You will realize that sticks and stones do break your
bones,
But words hurt longer.

Words are like knives,
Thrown by deadly murderers.
They cut deep,
Tearing pieces of you until no more is left,
Until you become an empty shell.

I mean,
Sticks and stones may break your bones,
But words will make your blood run cold,
Freeze the very depth of your soul,
Rip your heart into two,
Only to crush your spirit.

Words hurt,
Leave wounds that never heal,
And I don't just mean scratches,
I mean scars that stay,
Labels that never erase.

When you said those words to him/her,
Did you not think that they will cut deep?

Remain only to torture him/her?

Was he/she just a target for you knife practice?
When you held him/her up,
And tacked him with your labels,
Did you think that,
His/her armor will be strong enough to hold against it?

Why did you choose to be a murderer?
Hiding behind your steel cold knives of words?

I mean
Sticks and Stones may break bones,
But words are frozen knives,
That will decide the life of its victim.

Letters of the past and present me by Dorothy Adu-Amankwah

This poem is dedicated to the little girl I wished could have heard read it when she needed it most.

Age 4
The doctors told me that mom had a disease called stroke, so I wrote a letter to Mr. Stroke
Dear Stroke,
You have overshadowed mother
For three years now she has been your prisoner
You have infested her cells with your poison
So now, she stays trapped by you
No longer able to move with me, walk with me, or play with me
Tears become my breath when she coughs up blood in the middle of the night
My ears bleed at the ping-pong ping-pong of the ambulance as they come take her away
Loneliness fills my pillow with tears
So please give her back to me.
Thank you.
Bye-Bye mister Stroke

Age 7
I asked you to give her back to me,
Not to hand her to over to another warden that will put her soul into chains forever.
They told me that mom had gone to heaven,
But I knew better,

Mom was gone forever.
So now, here I am at the funeral.
They have warned me not to cry,
So, I guard my tears behind these glass doors,
And I am afraid that they will crack but I cannot speak
a word so
Steps like blocks
I pass my still mom
With each step, little pieces of me wither
And I am straining not to become ash,
But it's hard to stand when you have lost your heart.
I take my seat in a corner guarding these fragile tears
straining to break.

Age 16
A letter to the past me
Little girl,
I see you in a corner,
Struggling with a painful heart.
Don't hide behind being your tears.
Let them out, for there will be a time when they will be
too frozen to shed
Breath,
Even if the wounds in your heart make it painful.
Breath,
Even if you feel like you are breaking.
Breath,
For in time these wounds will heal.
I want you to know that you are strong,
Stronger than you ever imagined.
Know that everything will be okay in the end,
And if it is not okay then it is not the end.
Love, a future you

"This War Torn World" by Brandon VanderLaan

This War Torn World

                                                     It's Tearing

Itself Apart
This Very Earth, This Society We Are In
Generation After Generation
This War Torn World
Destroys Itself From The Inside Out
We All Must Stand Together
We All Must Link Hands
Help One Another
And Protect Each other
This War Torn World

It's Decomposing So Fast

But If We Work Together

We Can Recreate This World
Mold It Into A Better World
A Safer World, A Peaceful World
So Stand Firm

Hold Your Ground
Link Arms With The People Of This Earth
This War Torn World
Pick Up A Shovel To Clear Out The Rubble
Grab A Hammer And A Nail
And Lets Rebuild This Earth
This War Torn World
Together

The Caged Bird is Me by Brooke Parsons

The caged bird sings with the anticipation that
someone will hear its desperate call for freedom
It sings higher and higher, until the pitch is too high
even for dogs to hear it
The tempo rises and falls like the wind, just outside its
window

I know why the caged bird sings
For freedom, fresh air, and wind beneath its wings
But what I don't know is why it keeps trying day after
day, even though its freedom never comes

Its freedom is a key that hangs from the white hook,
beside the door to my freedom
But both key and door are far too high for me to reach,
so why do I keep trying
Why does the caged bird sing

The caged bird sings for freedom
And one day I will set it free
I watch it day after day
The caged bird has sad black dipped eyes
Get close enough and you can count the rings around
his eyes telling you how long he has suffered
I will set him free

But,
What will the caged bird do once he is free
Will it sing
The whole purpose for its voice was for his freedom

Will it cease to sing
Will it lose its voice

And for this reason I hate my human greed
For I long to hear its songs of sorrow because it made
me feel not alone

I sit in my cage, let him sit in his

Life is not fair
I use my voice to try to let others know my pain
But being a child, my song disappears into a field of
empty static, and I am ignored

So we will suffer together and share our songs of our
broken sorrow
And I will not let him go

"A Soul Like Mine" by Brandon VanderLaan

Dark as Night
Filled with Light
Stuffed with Lies
Full Of Truth
Stuck on the Ground
Yet Soars through the Sky
Nightmares Strike
Dreams Prevail
Tragedy Comes
And Hope Arises
Such a Wonderful thing
This Soul of Mine
It's Amazing isn't it
This Soul of Mine
And the Best part is
Everyone has One
A Strong Soul, a Loving Soul, a Unique Soul
It May be Hiding Deep Inside
But Everyone has One
A Soul Like Mine

The so called "sister" by Hannah Kim

So the so called "sister" is a very cute yet obnoxious one.
She can be a child at times but has the mentality of an adult.
Whatever I do, she either compliments or gives advice.
I feel small and oh yes very small whenever she says a compliment or advice.
Anyway, the bond between us is so strong and very durable that nothing nor anyone can tear it apart.
Sounds cheesy, huh?
This is an absolute truth.
If something or someone that tries to tear the bond apart, will have to pay a price.
Now you may say "What price?" and ill politely answer "The trust that we had betweens us sisters"
Without my sister or so called "sister" I would not be able to live as the older one and cry like a river on a bright, clear, beautiful night sky.
I love her dearly.
She is a like a jewel glistening on a sunny, warm day.
That jewel is very precious to me and I'll cherish it forever,
I love you my so called "sister"

Falls Church High School
Falls Church, Virginia

I'm Not a Poet by Zanasha Findley

I am not a poet!

Actually I don't know what I want to be called

I use to much of my mouth
And not enough of my mind
But I want this (head)
To have one of these (mouth)
So my thoughts can speak, to where they spit in your
face and hits you not here (head)
But here (heart)

I want my words to be so powerful that they take you
under
Gasping for air in my sea of words
Waves of verses keep knocking you off your feet
I want my words to make you weak.
Fall to your knees and unable to stand,
Crying out to be released from the oppression of my
violent words stomping all over your heart

But I don't want to be called a poet

My words aren't meant to be on paper,
They're meant to be dancing up here, with me, not to
entertain nor distract but coo to you to come and join
them.
Wrap yourself in these words
You may be thinking a blanket
But I'm thinking anaconda

Constricted construction of my persuasion that's
rolling off my sharp tongue

Don't call me a poet though

Instead come with me to the world where my thoughts
flow like rivers
But my words are the sun with no clouds of protection
A clear day to burn you with my annunciation and
watch you fry from my sentences
My river of thoughts may be your only salvation.
Cooling and collecting to tend to your wounds
So call me Poseidon, King of the flow!

This way you, as my audience, fear what I speak and
rush for my mind, the eye of the storm
My words are too violent so you wish to beat me at my
own game
Want to predict my next move so you can evade my
invasion of lyrics
But my plans are precise and my soldiers of style are
standing ready.
The battlefield is before me yet it too trembles at my
phrases
Ready to form from my fanatical fantasies!

Call me General Slasher because my words cut deep.
I'll run you through with my passionate paragraphs of
positively poisonous rhythm and vibe.

My thoughts though, are milk and honey.
Sweet and delectable...but when they transform

I begin to spew and spat words that drape over your senses.
Dropping bombs of venom that keep you gasping and suffocating
yet formulated from the nectar of my ideas.
Take cover in my mind;
Find comfort in the process of this "poet"

But hey! Don't call me that.

It's Ok by Zanasha Findley

Umm... this may sound weird...but,
Let's all get naked.
I know, I know, that sounds a bit umm... lewd?
But I'm not trying to be rude,
I'm just saying let's all get on the same level.

No shirt, no shoes, no shame.
Because we are all the same when flesh, blood, and
bone are all that matter.
We're Adams and Eves in the garden of life.
We might be meant to be at ease, yet we're deceived to
believe we're rotten
Because we're peeled away by the claims of our peers
And forced to swallow the sinful judgment which
attacks our core
Causing us to vomit seeds of doubt and sprout just
enough to retreat because we're growing on
insecurities.
Living Snow Whites as we bite this apple in spite of the
poison handed to us
As we baffle with sorrow and disgust upon ourselves.

But it's ok
Though the ground we stand on are promises, and yes
the fall hurts when they're broken,
But leave yourself open and clear.
After every piece of dirt is splattered on your name and
the glass may have shattered, but you'll claim to see
clearly
When the Windex of forgiveness is all you need.
It's ok.

So don't be clothed in such hate that it wears you,
Hangs you up to dry after you've cried a river in which
you've drowned in.
And pounds and pounds of makeup to cover those
scars,
And yes it's hard,
But it's ok.

Don't walk a runway of deceit in tattered rags as
though they were elegant garments
And as harmless as it may seem, I'd prefer to streak
down the street.
I'll be the first to go skinny dipping in a river of
compassion
Past the rapids of lies
Baptized in mercy to forgive those whose faults are
crimes in my eyes.
And it's ok if I YES I, am the first to say my birthday
suit suits, not only me, but you as well
So what do ya say,
Wanna get naked?

Love Child by Danny Tran

Everybody always told me I was a love child
For a long time I thought that was when my parents
love was so strong
That it became a tangible thing.....me
But then I went to high school and math told me I was
the product of a equation
The multiplication of my mom and dad
But my problem included the subtraction of birth
control
And the addition of a few beer plus another man
But in math you can only have one male
Because when I put it in my calculator it came out as
an error
The equivalent of a love child

So I am the mistake in the equation called a family
Since I was the outlier in this equation, maybe if I got
better in math
I could fix this problem so everything can add up
I worked endless days getting better in class and
brought home report card with A's to show dad But he
would just keep going on like infinity--nothing has
happened
I felt like pi
Because people see me just not all of me
Because they don't want to deal with everything that is
me
So they cut me to fit in there box--3.14
The pain stings like getting an F on a test
But I cover it up with ease because all the practice I've
done

Just like how I study for class

So I went to school with my mask looking how I
usually do
Like I was so happy and cheerful--nothing can bring
me down
So I went to my friends to have a chat when I realized
they're not really my real friends
I sit next to them hoping I won't feel as alone as I really
do
It doesn't work because they are just remainders
Left over after everybody divided in to groups
It hurts when they can't solve the variable that's me

I go home and I feel my hold on my parentheses start
to falter
They keep my fragile persona from crumbling
I see my dad and everything blurs
I end up in my room with my heart that is constricted,
With every heart filled sob that send tendrils of pain
racing thought my body till I'm numb
All I'm left with are my dark thoughts
I have no friends
Nobody loves me

But her
She is the other factor in my prime number showing
me I'm not alone
She is the pencil to my paper world showing me that
everything is not set in stone
Because when I told her that sometimes I wish that I
was not given this life

Her face cracks sending tears that make my world
tremble
Because she told me she can't be in this world without
me
Because we're the same--we're both negative
She told me I don't need to be a part of this equation
We can write our own and change these double
negatives in to a positive

I'm Not Ready by Isaiah Abadia

Giovanni Manz was the fastest in his platoon,
He was known as 'Supermanz'
In a place that doesn't tolerate individuality.
"Get back in your place, soldier 09692,
Get back in your place!"

Yes, come back to your place.
Come home so we can see your face one more time...
Because we're not ready for you to go.
I understand now what they mean when they say
'The pen is mightier than the sword'
But sometimes that pen becomes the sword,
Because when you sign on that dotted line,
All individuality is stripped away to serve a country
that doesn't even know your name.

You're relocated away from home
To these places called military bases
Where they restock on live soldiers to replace those
that expired out in the field.

When I find mom staining the carpet with her tears
from seeing your picture on the TV stand,
I know it isn't from the wonderful thought of you
serving your country.
It's from the thought that
One day,
One bullet,
Will just so happen to have found your brain,
Because, Superman, you're not bullet proof.

At night, she drowns her pillow with questions like
"What do you call a mother who doesn't have her
child?"
But I guarantee that her tears say everything she never
could
As she chokes and sobs into her pillow till she falls
asleep.
"Gio," she's saying... she's not ready.

It's as if a plaque and a picture of my dead brother is
supposed to make me feel better.
Yes, I'd LOVE to look at a picture that would remind
me of your funeral.
That day where someone finally tells me
"He's dead. And all we have left is his voice in our
head."

That picture of you dressed up in your uniform,
Sitting on my TV stand
Next to the flag of the country that praises your
services
But doesn't even know your name without looking at a
dog tag
When the kill was confirmed, like some Black Ops: Call
of Duty mission...
You can't respawn in this map,
You don't get another fight,
That bullet is your kryptonite.

"Soldier 09692," no.....
Soldier Giovanni Manz A.K.A. Supermanz.
Gio, you're not superman
And I'm not ready for you to go.

And trust me,
When I look into your eyes and say goodbye,
I can tell you don't even believe yourself when you say you'll be fine.
Because, no matter how Army Strong you get...
You're not ready...
You never will be...
And neither will we.

The Color Brown by Isaiah Abadia

"Ok class, today we're going to be painting a pretty
picture for Christmas time.
Be creative and use your imagination.
Make sure it's very colorful and at the end we're going to
hang them up for all to see.
But remember don't use any ugly colors, like Brown, or
else you'll ruin you painting."

From elementary school, we were taught that anything
Brown
Could only destroy everything visibly appealing to the
human race. Our ancestors molded and sculpted
memories and unforgotten dreams
Using only the finest shades and tones of Brown.
Sculptures no words could ever describe using the natural
hues of Earth.

This sculpture we are standing on wasn't built by my
people,
We are considered foreign to this land,
Even if Puerto Rico is a U.S. Territory.

Statistics will show that I am not destined to be the next
Steve Jobs or Steven Hawking
But instead, I will be the head..... of the custodians.
I'm not expected to graduate high school
But I will be expected to clean them.

I won't be making any grey graphite paintings with a
number 2 pencil in a college class or dorm room
So instead, my paintbrush will be a mop
And my soapy Fabuloso and bleach filled water will be my
paint

While I wash away the remains of my elementary school painting that was once destroyed,
All because I used the color Brown.

The only graph I might be near is the graph paper,
Trash paper, I picked up from under the desk
And when I look up "oh nice, more chewed gum" stuck to the bottom,
Creating its own painting in the empty classroom
Of the high school I'm not supposed to graduate from.

If I won't graduate then at least my parents can homeschool me,
Not teaching me how to get off the "darned grease stains" or how to get to those "hard to reach places" with as clean rag
But helping me get to the hard to reach place
Off the list of statistics and on to the list of students enrolling into a college class.

So, instead of being another number on a list of "you did your best" and "at least you tried,"
I'll be who my dog sees me as,
Because he sees in black and white.
I'll be the best person, the best painter,
And he will love me and all my paintings because I used the color brown.

Being a janitor is fine. I understand what they do because of what my parents have experienced.
I am thankful for custodians.
If I were to be a custodian I would be the Pablo Picasso of custodians.
But that is NOT the picture I'm destined to paint.

I Love You by Jason Reales

I love you.
It's all I can say when I think about you all day-I feel
crazy, no cray,
Because I'm ghetto, when I dance around in the
meadow in my head full of yellow dandelions, my heart
goes to high from low, but just so you know I'm not
high,
I'm just lucky enough to be the guy, who wakes up in
the middle of the night,
Saying how did I get so lucky to catch your eye, or
lucky enough to hold you tight
Whenever we have to say hi, or goodbye.

I love you.
Whenever I realize how much you mean to me, or
when I look around and see,
That all I see is you standing right next to me or when
I'm down and can't believe in life anymore, there you
are today, like the day before to hold my hand within
yours, when my head feels sore from all the pounding
of life knocking on my front door.

I love you.
When the words of those three words become found,
you won't head a sound
From my mouth, not till I've written down, every single
thought bound, to each and every memory wound
around my heart from the very start to today,
And every word I wanted to say to you, of every time
you made my mind fly away,

Into the sky like sun rays, to another planet in a distant place, to be alone,

With you of course, to let it be known, how much the love you've shown,

Has grown, into the sturdy bones that alleviate the stitches sewn,

To the one broken glass that cracked, from the overwhelming questions asked in class, "what's this?" and "what's that?", I Understand! And then you take my hand, and I lose the name brand from people who think they know who I am, and then I realize that your smile, takes me to another land, where all I see, I you, and me,

The Real Me.

1, 2, 3 by Mikalanne Paladino

1...2...3
They built my fence with three sides
Vertical
Horizontal
Horizontal
1...2...3
And you labeled me an "F"
Am I no more to you than three lines?
Three lines that I get to live in
Three lines that mean nothing but a title given to me
by the cyborgs of society assigning us an average to live
by I'm just a statistic that means nothing more to you
but a tally.

Because I don't want a part of your society Especially to
be one in a majority That's just not my place To live
within your carefully drawn lines When I know there
has to be more to me, to life Than a letter on a page.

You are not me
And I can't be you
I don't want to be an average
I don't want to just "get by"
I want to thrive.

Do you think that quite possibly
Maybe I'm more than "A" or a "B"?
And I don't have a future planned out you see So don't
you tell me how it's going be.

A...B...C can't by me happiness

And it won't teach me love
But if you want, give me an "F"
Since when was our identities decided by the alphabet
In Pre-K we were told that "F" was for Fragrant Flowers
and words like Freedom and Flight But now we have
"F" written upon our foreheads for "Future Failure."

When did "Land of the Free" become "Land of the
Freely Labeled"?
When did numbers and titles become more important
than happiness and love?
Why do we take more care crafting together blustering
essays about our routine lives when it was all for them,
So that they can pick and choose us like a kid
separating the good candy from the "bad"?
Why do we care what they think, what they want,
when it's all based on three stupid lines!?

You are not me
And I can't be you
I want to be more than some average that you think
you can mold "you care for me..."
Please.
How many more lies can be told?

1...2...3 lines!
Don't you see what you're placing on me?
My worth crumbles with just three lines!
It's so easy for you to kill me
And I haven't even gotten to live enough to yell "I'm
more than your pitiful 'F'!"

I can paint feelings of pain and love with a stroke of graphite I can portray worldly emotions upon a stage and move my audience to tears But you wouldn't know any of that because 1...2...3 I'm nothing!

Don't you tell me I'm not trying
Don't say "child" so condescending
I'm not so little and I have ideas bursting from the seams I see all this new perspective and all you see is routine.

You're not me
And I refuse to be you
And we are all our own routine
Not an average to be hacked down to size What's so wrong with wanting to be happy?

Curry Stain by Mikalanne Paladino

You know how you meet those people?
Especially that first person where you two just clicked,
Like two missiles locked onto the same target,
And when they hit...

Ha-ha screw the "love" metaphor
They freaking wreck each other.

You know your favorite restaurant?
The one on your birthday with your favorite dress,
The waiter brings your favorite curry dish...all down
your front,
And five years later the stain's still there?

Well you're my curry stain,
And the scar where the nuke struck,
I've evacuated the war zone,
And my dress lies crumpled in my closet in a dust
heap,
I avoid it every day,

But sometimes...
I get a bit sick or I catch a glimpse of stained lace.
The sickness is like a tug on the heart,
And the blurring of vision,
I'm so much better

But still I remember being broken,
I remember the destruction of all my functions,

When the blast of your "affections" happened to
radiate and poison.
The stain reminds me of that dinner,
I tasted and smelled so many different things
But I see the stain and remember what I ate,
I can feel the fat building beneath my skin,
No matter how hard I hit the gym,
You on my hips no longer on my lips.

You've stained me,
And you've nuked me,
All while not caring how I cared for you,
You still have a pull on me and I loathe you.
I loathe you so much!
You cannot comprehend.
I hate how I still will care,

Even if you nuke me,
How I will still try to comfort you when you break,
And make you see that you're not so hated,
Just really thoughtless decisions,
Just a push of a button and another innocent scarred.
"Move on!" you stupid girl!
Oh honey,
God knows I have,
He knows that I loathe you in the sweetest of ways,
Because you see...
You're the curry stain on my heart.

**Chantilly High School
Chantilly, Virginia**

Standing on the Ocean by Lina Snyder Romero

You have to believe it's not water. It is only... paper.
Paper- often the only one I trust not to talk through I
tape I mend its tears with
Paper- my personal washbasin to cleanse my soul and
let all my fears trickle into And away.
Paper- my self-prescribed therapy that often does more
hurt than help, savagely slicing my fingers when I try to
crumple it in frustration
And when I can no longer muffle my shriek of pain,
I am told to calm down, told it is only a paper-cut.
Nothing more.
I had pulled out my battered old map of the world
From a dark cavernous box adrift in a sea of packaging,
Its colorful star stickers that marked the passage of my
travels
Glowing through so brightly they burned with a painful
ache to go back,
I pushed those memories aside and took out a ruler.
Putting one end on where I'd been and the other on
where I was
I connected the two, building a bridge of plastic
between the two worlds.
My past and my present.
But everyone knows that plastic is fake,
And plastic won't last, not like the sturdy steel of the
plane that brought me here
So all I could do was play pretend for the moment.
Running my fingers up and down the bridge that
pierced the P in Pacific
P for purgatory, for limbo, for stuck in-between.

Centimeters on one side, inches on the other, caught in between
Like me.
If only there a half-way point. Was there?
 Quick contemplation later found me at nine and half inches.
Twenty-four centimeters.
And as my finger lingered, I soon realized that to be in between
I'd have to be standing on the ocean.

Sorry I'm Not You by Lina Snyder Romero

I can still remember the bewildered stares that
followed me
When I first reached for the shaker
Holding in my other hand the prized gold of my
childhood
Sweet as the success I hoped to one day make.
And as I salted my mango as I had done so many
countless times before,
I told them to try it, it's better than it sounds.
But I guess it was a little much, the contradictions
between salty and sweet
Can be a little hard to get used to.
Maybe I shouldn't have suggested it.
Maybe I shouldn't have done it at all, and made a
scene.
But how could I go back to doing things the way I once
had,
After I had tasted a life so much sweeter, and saltier
and more complex?
It was then that I heard the resounding slams
Of what seemed to be hundreds of people closing their
minds to me all at once.
Taking their children and hiding under the stairs
Watching in horrified fascination as the strange
specimen
Began to knock on their doors
Begging for someone to let her in until her knuckles
bled and then she cried.
Not because it hurt- well, not just because it hurt-
But because she didn't want to be the girl nobody let in

She wanted to be the girl who opens the door and says with a smile
"Can I help you?"

Most of the time, they didn't seem to want my help.
And it stung like a slap. The heart-jarring hexagon of stop,
Slow down, give it time, watch the signs.
I am done slowing down. Done waiting around,
Scanning the horizon for a time they'll understand.
Because the truth is, I am never looking straight ahead anymore.
When my head isn't up in the clouds, it's on the ground
Where all the details lay.
Where anyone who's ever been overstepped lays in wait for the next
Soul-crushing sole to hit them
And to those whose shoes supplied the ammunition for our humiliation
Who can never bring themselves to understand the mystique of a salted mango
I'm sorry I'm not you.

Hayfield Secondary School
Alexandria, Virginia

seasick by Sam Dickison

the truth is
leaving her was no "selfless act".
I was not trying to save her
from some horrid fate my cold heart
would bring-
I wanted to save myself
from a sinking ship

I knew that we would never be sailing
on calm waters
and I had grown tired with
the idea of being thankful for thunderstorms
simply because they are not hurricanes

I am not exaggerating when I say that we were
an romanticized suicide pact
sharing a wordless understanding that if one of us went
overboard
the other would follow-
not because we both wanted to die we just
didn't know how to live on our own anymore.
and the truth is
it took me months after we broke up
for me to believe I would not go to hell
for saving myself.
last week was the first time
I didn't have a panic attack when you spoke to me.
you reminded me I'd said i'd never leave
as if we both knew
that you would be the first to drown

untitled by Sam Dickison

They will ask for you to come out with them
or to call them
or to text

do not.

These opportunities will rise again.
Now you must learn
how to see your skin as the sun hits it,
you are reflecting moonlight over the mountains.
Surround yourself with succulents,
peonies and lavender,
allow the bees to be your friends
and watch the pollination.
Pollinate the idea of yourself as a flower in your mind:
You are a rose;
Delicate,
but ready to fight for yourself.
Now
you must learn to fight for yourself.
To only strike against those trying to hurt you,
to stop trying to hurt yourself.
Today,
the sun will grace your skin
and you will watch the plants grow,
today you will give yourself
room to grow.

Metamorphosis by Judy Russell

Followed forever by a shadow,
the spider's skin stunk of rot and mold.
Born without humor,
a mute never to hear heaven's music.
Death would not embrace her lightly,
her malleability was immortality.

Her endless webs
stretched across the world
weaving words through tongues and brains.
She gave the moon dimples, to smile
And the sun, hair to shine.

But don't be mistaken by her looks
Spite is her lover,
And metamorphosis flows through her blood.

The edge of the earth by Judy Russell

The future is a giant,
wringing the vacant bodies of ambition.
In a haste to become the past,
it locks its corrupt secrets with every sunset
and grows thicker with every sunrise.
The endless alliteration of a clock
overflows our days,
day by day, hour by hour, minute by minute.
The present remains naïve,
Truly unsure of itself.

30545686R00058

Made in the USA
Charleston, SC
19 June 2014